Ready, Steady, Rap

Ready, Steady, Rap

Rap poems
collected by John Foster

OXFORD
UNIVERSITY PRESS

OXFORD

UNIVERSITY PRESS

Great Clarendon Street, Oxford OX2 6DP

Oxford University Press is a department of the University of Oxford.
It furthers the University's objective of excellence in research, scholarship,
and education by publishing worldwide in

Oxford New York

Athens Auckland Bangkok Bogotá Buenos Aires
Cape Town Chennai Dar es Salaam Delhi Florence Hong Kong Istanbul
Karachi Kolkata Kuala Lumpur Madrid Melbourne Mexico City Mumbai
Nairobi Paris São Paulo Shanghai Singapore Taipei Tokyo Toronto Warsaw

with associated companies in Berlin Ibadan

British Library Cataloguing in Publication Data available

ISBN 0-19-276280-X

1 3 5 7 9 10 8 6 4 2

Typeset by Mary Tudge (Typesetting Services)

Printed in the UK by Cox & Wyman Ltd, Reading, Berkshire

Contents

Rapping

Rapping on the window
Rapping on the door
Wrapping up the presents
Wrapping paper on the floor.

Wrapping up in winter
Wrapping up a game
Wrapping round a chocolate
That is rapping that's a pain.

But rapping on the radio
Or rapping in the street
Is rapping with an attitude
And rapping that is neat!

Daniel Phelps

The Schoolkids' Rap

Miss was at the blackboard writing with the chalk,
When suddenly she stopped in the middle of her
   talk.
She snapped her fingers—snap! snap! snap!
Pay attention, children, and I'll teach you how to
   rap.

She picked up a pencil, she started to tap.
All together, children, now, clap! clap! clap!
Just get the rhythm, just get the beat.
Drum it with your fingers, stamp it with your feet.

That's right, children, keep in time.
Now we've got the rhythm, all we need is the
   rhyme.
This school is cool. Miss Grace is ace.
Strut your stuff with a smile on your face.

Snap those fingers, tap those toes.
Do it like they do it on the video shows.
Flap it! Slap it! Clap! Snap! Clap!
Let's all do the schoolkids' rap!

John Foster

Stock Cupboard Rap

In our teacher's stock cupboard
With his paper and pens,
Lurk all sorts
Of his peculiar friends.

> Large and small, fat and thin,
> You'd better watch out if you need to go in!

There's a little brown hairy one
That lives on the floor,
And will bite your leg
When you come through the door!

> Large and small, fat and thin,
> You'd better watch out if you need to go in!

The long thin furry one
Sits on the shelf,
Show him a mirror
And he'd frighten himself!

> Large and small, fat and thin,
> You'd better watch out if you need to go in!

The teeny black fuzzy one
Hides among the pens,
With fangs like that
He hasn't many friends!

Large and small, fat and thin,
You'd better watch out if you need to go in!

But the hairiest, scariest creature of all
Clings like a limpet up on the wall.
When you creep inside he stretches his limbs,
And tickles your head, among other things!

Large and small, fat and thin,
You'd better watch out if you need to go in!

So take great care if you have to find
A pencil, a rubber, or a pen of some kind.
To go in that cupboard takes nerves of steel,
Cos if one doesn't get you—
ANOTHER ONE WILL!!

Anne Logan

Gareth's Greatest Goal

I whisk the ball out to the wing
The crowd goes wild, hear them sing.

I swoop behind a flat back four
Everyone's yelling, 'Go on, score!'

Just the goalie now to beat
I fox him with my flashing feet.

Push the ball into the net
My hat-trick goal, the best one yet.

YE-E-E-E-SSSSSSSS!!!!!!

The crowd go crazy, what a riot
Then suddenly it's very quiet.

I look around, I'm standing up
And this is not the FA Cup.

It's my classroom and class three
Are staring open-mouthed at me.

It seems I've had some kind of dream
Winning for my favourite team.

And now I've yelled and shouted out
Pulled off my shirt and jumped about.

My teacher laughs, shakes his head
As I start to blush bright red.

'OK,' he says, 'my lesson's boring
And with all these goals you're scoring

I must admit that I'm impressed
But, Gareth, son, please get dressed.'

David Harmer

The Lunchtime Slip Slop Rap

This is the lunchtime slip slop rap
Spaghetti hoops or sausage in a bap
Click your fingers, stamp your feet
Groovy gravy, two veg, no meat,
Shake your body, swivel those hips,
Salt and vinegar, fish and chips
Hold your hands up in the air
Chocolate custard, apple or pear
Feel that beat, you're on the loose
Lemonade or orange juice,
Chatter clatter, make a noise
No more hungry girls and boys
Rhythm and rap to the roasting rhyme.
Lunch is done, it's playtime.

Andrew Fusek Peters

King Andy

Andy Curtis is
The break dance king
Watch him swivel
Watch him swing.
Light on his feet as
A butterfly in jeans
He can hip-hip-hop
Like a jumping bean.

'Yo, Andy! Go, Andy!'
Everybody shouts
As his hands hit the tarmac
And his feet shoot out.
Wrists like steel
Curvy as a snake
Shrugs his shoulders
Shimmies and shakes.

He's the break dance
break dance
break dance king
And he
Rules the playground when he
does his thing.

Patricia Leighton

The Easy PC Rap

All the kids in our class
sing the Easy PC Rap,
since we caught that dinner lady
in the Easy PC trap.

Always bossing, always nagging,
always putting us kids down,
that dinner lady told on
anyone who fooled around.

So, we got the new computer
and we wished a wicked wish,
that our lady would go cyber
and what happened was delish!

One minute she was scowling,
and looking really mean
then the next she's yelling at us
from behind the PC screen!

That bossy dinner lady
looks as sick as any chip
cos she knows that we'll delete her
if she gives us any lip.

She can flap her nylon overall
and stamp her bossy boots,
we just click the exit button—
wow—this PC's really cute!

OK, we're meanie-beanies,
we should let her out the trap,
then we think of all that bossing . . .
sing the Easy PC Rap!

Maureen Haselhurst

TV Rap

After school
what suits me
is to sit on the carpet
and watch TV.

Watch TV
Watch TV
I sit on the carpet
and watch TV.

I burst in
about half past three.
Kick off my shoes
and get comfy.

Get comfy
Get comfy
I kick off my shoes
and get comfy.

Dad says, 'You're too near.
Take my advice.
Move further back
or you'll damage your eyes.'

But my eyes don't hurt
and they haven't turned square.
Close to the screen
is what I prefer.

When I get home
what pleases me
is to sit on the carpet
and watch TV.

I watch TV
I watch TV
and I don't budge
until it's time for tea.

Time for tea
Time for tea
I don't budge
until it's time for tea.

Bernard Young

Little Sister

That's my little sister
Just five minutes old
Already seeking something
To bite and chew and hold,
That's my little sister
Already going bald
I can't just call her sister
So what will she be called?

I want to call her Carol
But all carols are hymns
I want to call her Jimmy
But I always visit gyms,
I want to call her spotty
But she may punch my nose
I will not call her Rosy
She don't look like a rose.

When I hear her crying
I want to call her *loud*
If she's the type for talking
I may call her a *crowd,*
If she's good at singing
I'll call her *nightingale*
If she keeps on grinning
She'll make the doctors wail.

The doctors called her beauty
But beauty is a horse
The nurses called her cutey
Being polite of course,
My mummy and my daddy
Just don't have an idea
We don't have a name ready
But we're so glad she's here.

Benjamin Zephaniah

Baby Rap!

Adults go gooey with a baby on their lap,
it's the cootchy-coo, cuddly-poo baby rap.

> Woopsy, poopsy, honey bun,
> sweetie, tweetie, sugar plum,
> snuggums, diddums, cutesie tootsie,
> bunnikins, honeykins, footsie wootsie.

Out on the street adults push their buggies,
desperate for coos and lots of huggies.
When baby cries; time to change that nap,
parents smile for it's their time to rap!

> Woopsy, poopsy, honey bun,
> sweetie, tweetie, sugar plum,
> snuggums, diddums, cutesie tootsie,
> bunnikins, honeykins, footsie wootsie.

Adults enjoy being a patter chatterbox
with 'precious, izzums, bless your cotton socks.'
So when babies cry, 'daddeeee, mummeeee,'
all adults do is shove in a dummy!

> Woopsy, poopsy, honey bun,
> sweetie, tweetie, sugar plum,
> snuggums, diddums, cutesie tootsie,
> bunnikins, honeykins, footsie wootsie.

Babies must wonder what's happening here,
all this cooey talk dribbling in their ear.
Those adults so noisy and full of prattle
perhaps their mouths should be stuffed with a
    RATTLE!

   Woopsy, poopsy, honey bun,
   sweetie, tweetie, sugar plum,
   snuggums, diddums, cutesie tootsie,
   bunnikins, honeykins, footsie wootsie.

Adults go gooey with a baby on their lap,
it's the cootchy-coo, cuddly-poo baby rap!

Ian Souter

If I Had a Brudda

If I had a brudda,
I would call my brudda Brad.
Brad'd be the greatest brudda
anybody had.
Brad'd drive me in his car.
Brad'd teach me pool.
Brad'd beat up any kid
that boddered me at school.
Brad'd give me money
and he'd praise me to our dad.
I wish I had a brudda like
imaginary Brad.

Loris Lesynski

Gran Can You Rap?

Gran was in her chair she was taking a nap
When I tapped her on the shoulder to see if she
  could rap.
Gran, can you rap? Can you rap? Can you, Gran?
And she opened one eye and said to me, man,
  I'm the best rapping Gran this world's ever seen
  I'm a tip-top, slip-slap, rap-rap queen.

And she rose from her chair in the corner of the
  room
And she started to rap with a bim-bam-boom,
And she rolled up her eyes and she rolled round
  her head
And as she rolled by this is what she said,
  I'm the best rapping Gran this world's ever seen
  I'm a nip-nap, yip-yap, rap-rap queen.

Then she rapped past my dad and she rapped past
  my mother,
She rapped past me and my little baby brother.
She rapped her arms narrow she rapped her arms
  wide,
She rapped through the door and she rapped
  outside.
  She's the best rapping Gran this world's ever seen
  She's a drip-drop, trip-trap, rap-rap queen.

She rapped down the garden she rapped down the
    street,
The neighbours all cheered and they tapped their
    feet.
She rapped through the traffic lights as they turned
    red
As she rapped round the corner this is what she
    said,
  I'm the best rapping Gran this world's ever seen
  I'm a flip-flop, hip-hop, rap-rap queen.

She rapped down the lane she rapped up the hill,
And as she disappeared she was rapping still.
I could hear Gran's voice saying, Listen, man,
Listen to the rapping of the rap-rap Gran.
  I'm the best rapping Gran this world's ever seen
  I'm a—
      tip-top, slip-slap,
        nip-nap, yip-yap,
          hip-hop, trip-trap,
            touch yer cap,
              take a nap,
                happy, happy, happy, happy,
                rap—rap—queen.

Jack Ousbey

April Fool Rap

There's a blob on your nose,
a smutch on your cheek,
and it looks as if your shoes
have just sprung a leak.

Chorus:
Try not to look.
Try to keep cool.
Don't let them make you
an April Fool.

There's a hole in your trousers,
a splotch on your hat.
Look out behind you—
a giant rat!

Chorus:
Try not to look.
Try to keep cool.
Don't let them make you
an April Fool.

There's a beetle on your collar.
There's a spider in your hair.
Don't sit down,
there's a snake on your chair.

Chorus:
Try not to look.
Try to keep cool.
Don't let them make you
an April Fool.

There's a bear at the window,
and there by the door
what's that knocking?
It's a d-d-dinosaur!

A dinosaur knocking,
did I hear you say?
Then you're the April Fool
cos it's past midday!

Tony Mitton

29

Visit to the Dentist Rap

Going to the dentist is the only time that boys
Have to open up their mouths—but not make a
   noise
But the dentist keeps talking about family and
   school
And all you can say is, 'Uh—oh—ool.'
You lie on your back looking straight up his nose
And at his Adam's Apple as up and down it goes.
He's poking in your mouth with a mirror on a stick
And another funny thing like a bent toothpick
Which he prods at your teeth and scrapes a bit
Until he says, 'That's fine. You can rinse and spit.'
You leap from the chair feeling fine
Now it's all over—until the next time.

John Coldwell

The Holiday Rap

I'm bopping round the beach
in my holiday cap
with my bucket and my spade.
It's the holiday rap.
Let the jellyfish wobble
and the crabs snip snap
but they can't catch me
that cool, rapping chap.
Let the flatfish flop
and the seagulls screech
I'm rap, rap, rapping
down the beach.
Bring the ice creams on
and the fish and chips
I want those flavours
on my lips.
Let the cold winds blow
and the sea slip slap,
I'll be out there doing
my holiday rap.

Marian Swinger

Roller Coaster Rap

Jump   on the   roller coaster
Hey, man, go!
       A press
               of the button
and we move off slow.

Pickin' up, pickin' up, pickin' up speed,
       now we're flying
               higher than the trees.

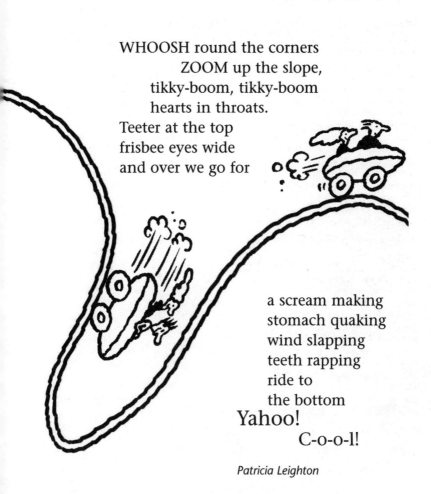

WHOOSH round the corners
ZOOM up the slope,
tikky-boom, tikky-boom
hearts in throats.
Teeter at the top
frisbee eyes wide
and over we go for

a scream making
stomach quaking
wind slapping
teeth rapping
ride to
the bottom
Yahoo!
C-o-o-l!

Patricia Leighton

The Palace Rap

There once was a queen
as proud as can be.
She was filled to the brim
with dignity.

Until a drummer
from a distant land,
came to play
in the royal band.

And he played with a pitter
and a pit-pit-pat.
And he played with a rappety
rat-tat-tat.

And the queen she heard
in the drum's wild beat,
something that made her
tap her feet.

And her feet went a-tapping,
and her hands went a-clapping,
and she said,
'I'm the queen
who's going to go a-rapping.'

So she rapped with a pitter
and a pit-pit-pat.
And she rapped with a rappety
rat-tat-tat.

She rapped round the ballroom.
She rapped round the throne.
But she didn't
like a-rapping
all on her own.

So the pageboy,
the footman,
the cook and the maid,
rapped around the palace
all that day.

And they rapped
out into
the palace yard,
just in time for
the Changing of the Guard.

And the soldiers
threw their caps
in the air,
and they rapped up and down
Trafalgar Square.

And the tourists,
the shoppers,
and the city folk, too,
all said, 'What fun,
let's join in, too!'

So they rapped with a pitter
And a pit-pit-pat.
And they rapped with a rappety
rat-tat-tat.

And they rapped all day
and they rapped all night.
And you never ever saw
such a pit-pat-rip-rap
pitter-patter-ripper-rapper
rappety-clappety-rip-rap sight!

Cynthia Rider

Guess What?

Nick nack lip smack
I'm the giant Beanstalk Jack
Nick nack lip smack
Children are my favourite snack
Nick nack lip smack
I gobble gobble nick-a-nack
Nick nack lip smack
Guess what is in my luncheon pack!

Debjani Chatterjee

It's Cool, Jack, It's Cool!

Did you hear the tale of this dude called Jack
who went for a walk up a mountain track?
Now he took a bucket and his girlfriend Jill
and he aimed to get to the top of the hill.
But the hill was steep, and the top was high
and I bet that Jack got to wonder why
that the well was built at the top of the pile,
for I heard that it always made Jill smile.

For she was a girl who was clever and slick.
She was a girl who caught on quick.
She remembered the things her school had taught
    her
and one was a fact about hill water.
Now Jill was trained as an engineer
she wasn't the type to scoff or sneer
and she certainly wasn't no mountaineer.
But she knew her physics and made it clear
water left to itself will naturally fall
and nobody needed that well at all!

Still, Jack didn't mind his mountain trek
but he sure didn't want to break his neck.
And though Jill didn't know, and it didn't show,
Jack had a problem with vertigo.
When he turned around and saw the drop
it made his poor heart almost stop.
It made him giddy, it made him sick
and he fell down the hill again mighty quick!

Now Jack held the bucket and for all we know
Jill held it too, and she wouldn't let go!
So Jack and Jill came tumbling down
and when they hit the bottom, Jack broke his
    crown.
Now Jack was feeling pretty sore
but it didn't stop Jill from laying down the law.
'We'll let the river bring the water down,
and we'll live in a semi in the middle of town.'

So Jill had her way, I'm glad to say,
and they've lived in that house until today.
No more climbing with buckets or pails,
they just turn on a tap . . . it never fails!

Brenda Williams

Goldilocks' Rap

Hey there, Big Bear,
What d'you like for breakfast?
Cornflakes, rice cakes,
Weetabix, or what?

I LIKE PORRIDGE!
GIVE ME PORRIDGE!
I LIKE A LOT OF PORRIDGE IN A
GREAT BIG POT!

Hey there, Mama Bear,
What d'you like to sit in?
Arm chair, deck chair,
Rocking chair, or what?

I LIKE MY CHAIR,
MY SIT-AND-SHUT-YOUR-EYE CHAIR,
MY-WATCH-THE-WORLD-GO-BY CHAIR,
I LIKE MY CHAIR A LOT.

Hey there, Baby Bear,
What d'you like to sleep in?
Bath tub, coal bin,
Flower bed, or what?

THAT'S REAL EASY!
IT'S EASY SQUEEZY WHEEZY!
THERE'S NOTHING IN THE WORLD
TO BEAT MY OWN SMALL COT!

Hey there, Three Bears!
What d'you think of Goldilocks?

BOOOOOOOOOO!

Kaye Umansky

The Fox and the Crow

Now this is the story
of the fox who saw
a piece of cheese
on the forest floor.

And that fox he hopped
up and down with glee,
and he said,
'Oh my,
this cheese is for me!'

But before that fox
could blink his eyes,
a big black crow
came whizzing by.

And she took that cheese
up into a tree.
And the fox said,
'Man,
there goes my tea!'

But that fox was as sly
as a fox can be.
So he went
and stood
underneath the tree.

And he said,
'Oh my!
What a beautiful crow!
Your eyes they glisten,
they glint, they glow.

'Your feathers
all shine,
and your beak is sleek.
Oh, how I wish
I could hear you speak.

'Or better still,
I wish you'd sing.
For a bird like you
could sing for a king.

'Dear crow!
Sweet crow!
Oh, beautiful crow!
Please sing for me,
it would please me so.'

So the crow went
'CAW!'
and the fox he saw
that cheese fall down
to the forest floor.

'Oh no!'
said the crow.
'I've been taken in!'
'Quite right,'
said the fox,
with a nasty grin.

And he ran
straight back
to his cosy den.
And the crow never fell
for that trick again!

Cynthia Rider

Rocking Rabbits

I was walking in the moonlight,
I was walking through the wood,
When I saw the strangest sort of sight
A person ever could.
There were rabbits in the clearing
There were rabbits round the trees
There were rocking, rapping rabbits,
Twitching noses in the breeze.
There were rabbits from the pet shops,
From the gardens, from the moors,
There were rabbits used to hutches,
There were those who lived outdoors.
There were black and white and grey and brown,
With spots and patches too,
There were dwarf and large, with ears that trailed,
And rabbits meant for stew.
They were rocking, they were rolling,
They were leaping high as kites
On this
Hippy, hoppy,
Flippy, floppy,
Rocking Rabbit Rave-up Night.

Daphne Kitching

Reindeer Rap

Well, it's Christmas Eve,
December 24th,
And we're on our way down
From the far, far north.
We got Santa in the sleigh
With a load of Christmas cheer,
We'll deliver the presents
Santa's worked on all year,
So if you think you hear a noise
When you're tucked up in bed,
A sorta scritch-scritch-scratching
Up above your head,
If you hear somebody tapping
Way up there on your roof
It'll just be the pawing
Of a reindeer hoof!
We'll be rapping on the rooftop,
We'll be rapping on the floor,
We'll be rapping on the window,
We'll be rapping on the door!
It's no problem towing Santa
Through the dark and snowy skies
But when he's drinking sherry wine
And eating all those mince pies
We get bored and lonely
And we wanna let him know
There's still a job to do—

Hey, man, we really gotta go!
No offence to all you people,
Just a word in your ear—
Maybe you could leave some carrots
For his cool REIN-DEER!
Or
We'll be rapping on the rooftop,
We'll be rapping on the floor,
We'll be rapping on the window,
We'll be rapping on the DOOR!

Sue Cowling

Dirty Dog Boogie

I **had** a dirty dog
    and I **had** a dirty cat
and I **took** them both to
    the laundromat.

The cat objected
    and the dog complained
so I took them home
    in the pouring rain.

The cat got mad
    but the cat got clean
and the dog was as shiny
    as I'd ever seen!

So even though they yell
    and even though they yowl
I take them in the rain
    and I take along a towel.

If you have a dirty dog
    and you have a dirty cat
don't take them
    don't take them
        don't take them to the laundromat.

Loris Lesynski

Duck Rap

Hey, chuck,
I'm a duck
Don't mistake
Me for a drake
I'm fond
Of my pond
I'm out in all weathers
In my waterproof feathers
I speak
Through my beak
Just quack, quack, quack
Is my backing track
I've only got one thought in my head
That's to paddle to the tourists who are throwing
    bread
Been doing my thing since I hatched from the egg
I don't work—I just borrow and beg
Then I waddle on my webbed feet back to the nest
Tuck my head in my feathers and take a rest.

John Coldwell

Dinosaur Stomp

I thought I saw
a Dinosaur
buy a pair of slippers
in a big shoe store
I asked him what
he bought them for
and he told me
his paw was sore
and what's more
began to roar
and showed me what
his teeth were for.

I ran like mad
across the floor
and bolted through
the shoe-store door
and nevermore
no nevermore
laughed out loud
at a Dinosaur.

David Harmer

Rappin' Rat

Rappin' rat, groovin' down the street
clappin' his paws to the rappin' beat.
Shivering his whiskers, shuffling his feet
Rappin' rat, groovin' down the street.

Rappin' rat, groovin' down the street
clappin' his paws, when who does he meet?
Just around the corner . . . Ratcatcher Pete!

So it's . . .
    . . . over the wall . . .
        down through the drain.

            'Ratcatcher Pete won't catch me again!

Ratcatcher Pete won't catch me!
This cool rat is gonna stay free!'

    Squeezing through the letterbox,
        sneaking up the stairs,
            scrambling over tables,
                scuttling under chairs.

Out through the back door,
doesn't miss a beat.
Rappin' rat is back on the street!

Rappin' rat, groovin' down the street
clappin' his paws to the rappin' beat.
Shivering his whiskers, shuffling his feet
Rappin' rat—the king of the street.

Maddy Morgan

The Boneyard Rap

This is the rhythm
of the boneyard rap,
knuckle bones click
and hand bones clap,
finger bones flick
and thigh bones slap,
when you're doing the rhythm
of the boneyard rap.
    Wooooooooooooooo!

It's the boneyard rap
and it's a scare.
Give your bones a shake-up
if you dare.
Rattle your teeth
and waggle your jaw
and let's do the boneyard rap
once more.

This is the rhythm
of the boneyard rap,
elbow bones clink
and backbones snap,
shoulder bones chink
and toe bones tap,
when you're doing the rhythm
of the boneyard rap.
    Woooooooooooooooo!

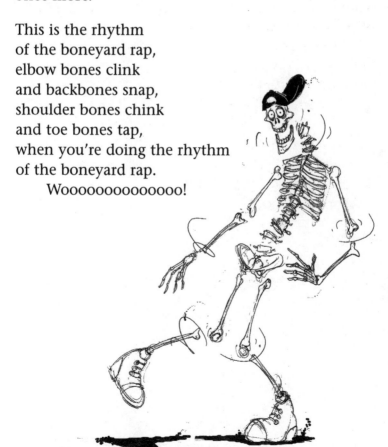

It's the boneyard rap
and it's a scare.
Give your bones a shake-up
if you dare.
Rattle your teeth
and waggle your jaw
and let's do the boneyard rap
once more.

This is the rhythm
of the boneyard rap,
ankle bones sock
and arm bones flap,
pelvic bones knock
and knee bones zap,
when you're doing
   the rhythm
of the boneyard rap.
   Woooooooooooooooo!

Wes Magee

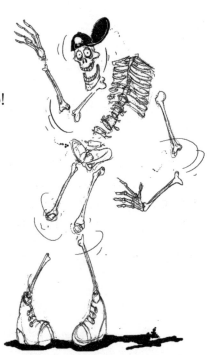

Witch in the Supermarket

There's a witch in the supermarket over there
After Fowler's treacle for her flyaway hair,
Buying up nail-varnish—black or green?
Rooting in the freezer for toad ice-cream!

There's a witch in the supermarket next row on
Asking where the Tinned Bats' Ears have gone,
Mutters 'Why do they always change things round?
Mouse Tails and Rat's Tongues can't be found!'

There's a witch in the supermarket down that aisle
Searching for something to blacken her smile,
She's a trolley full of tins for her witch's cat
Who simply swears by Bit-o-Bat.

Times are difficult and Bovril has to do
Instead of newt's blood for a tasty stew;
Sun-dried blue-bottles crunchy and sweet
Desiccated spiders for a Hallowe'en treat.

There's a witch in the supermarket at the till
Scribbling her cheque with a grey goose quill!
There's a witch at the check-out, look, Mum, quick!
Piling up her shopping on a big broomstick!

Angela Topping

The Most Important Rap

I am an astronaut
I circle the stars
I walk on the moon
I travel to Mars
I'm brave and tall
There is nothing I fear
And I am the most important person here.

I am a teacher
I taught you it all
I taught you why your
spaceship doesn't fall
If you couldn't read or write
where would you be?
The most important person here is me.

Who are you kidding?
Are you taking the mick?
Who makes you better
when you're feeling sick?
I am a doctor
and I'm always on call
and I am more important than you all.

But I'm your mother
Don't forget me
If it wasn't for your mother
where would you be?
I washed your nappies
and changed your vest
I'm the most important
and Mummy knows best.

I am a child
and the future I see
and there'd be no future
if it wasn't for me
I hold the safety
of the planet in my hand
I'm the most important
and you'd better understand.

Now just hold on
I've a message for you all
Together we stand
and divided we fall
so let's make a circle
and all remember this
Who's the most important?

EVERYBODY IS!

Roger Stevens

Ready, Steady, Rap!

Rap with your fingers. Rap with your toes.
Rap very gently with your knees and your nose.
Rap with your father. Rap with your mother.
Rap with your sister and your little baby brother.
Rap with your grandad. Rap with your gran.
Rap with the Knick-Knack Paddywack Man.
Rap when it's raining. Rap when it's fine.
Rap dancing in a circle or marching in a line.
Rap in the summer, in the autumn, in the spring.
Rap in the winter when hailstones sting.
Rap playing football, about to score a goal.
Rap with Georgie Porgie. Rap with Old King Cole.
Rap with Humpty Dumpty. Rap with Cinderella.
Rap with Mary Poppins and her flying umb(e)rella.
Rap with Willie Winkie as he's racing through the town.
Rap with Jack and rap with Jill, who's mending poor
Jack's crown.
Rap with the Duke of York and those ten thousand men.
They rapped right up to the top of the hill, and rapped
right down again.
Rap with your black friends. Rap with your white.
Rap in the daytime, and rap all through the night.
Get ready steady rapping,
With feet and hands a-tapping.
Then soon we'll have the rap
On the wicked world-wide map!

John Kitching

Index of titles/first lines
(First lines in italic)

ACKNOWLEDGEMENTS

We are grateful for permission to reproduce the following poems:

Loris Lesynski: 'Dirty Dog Boogie' and 'If I Had a Brudda' from *Dirty Dog Boogie* (Annick Press Ltd, 1999), reprinted by permission of the publishers. **Anne Logan:** 'Stock Cupboard Rap', copyright © Anne Logan 1999, first published in Paul Cookson (ed): *Unzip Your Lips Again* (Macmillan Children's Books, 1999), reprinted by permission of the author. **Wes Magee:** 'The Boneyard Rap' from *The Boneyard Rap and Other Poems* (Hodder Wayland, 2000) copyright © Wes Magee 2000, reprinted by permission of the author. **Jack Ousbey:** 'Gran Can You Rap?', copyright © Jack Ousbey 1993, first published in John Foster (ed): *All in the Family* (OUP, 1993), reprinted by permission of the author. **Ian Souter:** 'Baby Rap!', copyright © Ian Souter 1993, first published in David Orme (ed): *Doin Mi Ed In* (Macmillan Children's Books, 1993), reprinted by permission of the author. **Roger Stevens:** 'The Most Important Rap', copyright © Roger Stevens 1996, first pubished in Brian Moses (ed): *Performance Poems* (Southgate, 1996), reprinted by permission of the author. **Angela Topping:** 'Witch in the Supermarket', copyright © Angela Topping 1990, first published in *The Bees Knees* (Stride, 1990), reprinted by permission of the author. **Kaye Umansky:** 'Goldilocks' Rap', copyright © Kaye Umansky 1994, first published as 'Goldilocks and the Three Bears' in *Three Singing Pigs* (A & C Black, 1994), reprinted by permission of the author. **Benjamin Zephaniah:** 'Little Sister' from *Talking Turkeys* (Viking, 1994), copyright © Benjamin Zephaniah 1994, reprinted by permission of Penguin Books Ltd.

All other poems are published for the first time in this collection by permission of their authors.

Debjani Chatterjee: 'Guess What?', copyright © Debjani Chatterjee 2001. **John Coldwell:** 'Duck Rap' and 'Visit to the Dentist Rap', copyright © John Coldwell 2001. **Sue Cowling:** 'Reindeer Rap', copyright © Sue Cowling 2001. **John Foster:** 'The Schoolkids' Rap', copyright © John Foster 2001. **David Harmer:** 'Gareth's Greatest Goal' and 'Dinosaur Stomp', copyright © David Harmer 2001. **Maureen Haselhurst:** 'The Easy PC Rap', copyright © Maureen Haselhurst 2001. **Daphne Kitching:** 'Rocking Rabbits', copyright © Daphne Kitching 2001. **John Kitching:** 'Ready, Steady, Rap!', copyright © John Kitching 2001. **Patricia Leighton:** 'King Andy' and 'Roller Coaster Rap', copyright © Patricia Leighton 2001. **Tony Mitton:** 'April Fool Rap', copyright © Tony Mitton 2001. **Maddy Morgan:** 'Rappin Rat', copyright © Michael Morgan and Maddy Stewart 2001. **Andrew Fusek Peters:** 'The Lunchtime Slip Slop Rap', copyright © Andrew Fusek Peters 2001. **Daniel Phelps:** 'Rapping', copyright © Daniel Phelps 2001. **Cynthia Rider:** 'The Palace Rap' and 'The Fox and the Crow', copyright © Cynthia Rider 2001. **Marian Swinger:** 'The Holiday Rap', copyright © Marian Swinger 2001. **Brenda Williams:** 'It's Cool, Jack, It's Cool', copyright © Brenda Williams 2001. **Bernard Young:** 'TV Rap', copyright © Bernard Young 2001

Inside illustrations by:

Theresa Tibbetts

Chris Mould

Ellis Nadler